CELEBRATING THE LEGEND,
STEPHEN CURRY

_____

THIS BOOK BELONGS TO A LEGEND.

A STORY
INSPIRED BY STEPHEN CURRY

CONTROL YOUR WABA

WRITTEN BY:
JEFFREY DEVINE

ILLUSTRATED BY:
TIYE SAMONE

Jeffrey Devine
42808 Christy Street Suite 116
Fremont, CA 94538

ISBN-PAPERBACK : 979-8-378-30693-0
ISBN-eBOOK: 979-8-218-15328-1

Illustrated and produced by Phase Creative Studios LLC.
www.phasecreativestudios.com

For information regarding special discounts for bulk purchases, please contact Jeffrey Devine at (858) 775-6137.

THIS BOOK IS DEDICATED TO EVERYONE
ASPIRING TO BE A LEGEND.

LEARN TO CONTROL YOUR WABA, AND ANYTHING
YOU CAN IMAGINE IS YOURS FOR THE TAKING.

YOU ARE TRULY LEGENDARY. THANK YOU!

TABLE OF CONTENTS

GUIDE TO CONTROLLING YOUR WABA

PROLOGUE
STEPHEN CURRY

AT 6' 3", STEPHEN CURRY IS NO GIANT BY NBA STANDARDS, BUT NO PLAYER IN ITS' HISTORY HAS CHANGED THE GAME MORE.

TODAY, MORE KIDS LOOK UP TO STEPHEN CURRY THAN ANY OTHER PLAYER IN THE NBA. HIS UNIQUE IMPACT HAS INSPIRED THE WAY CHILDREN PLAY TODAY.

THERE ARE KIDS ACROSS THE GLOBE, EMULATING HIS STYLE BY SPORTING HIS LEAD SELLING JERSEYS. VISIT ANY PLAYGROUND AND SEE FOR YOURSELF!

In addition to revolutionizing the game of basketball, Stephen Curry is also a father of three. Like other families, the Curry's face parenting challenges.

During a recent interview, Curry shared his WABA parenting principle as a solution. WABA stands for words, actions, behavior and attitude.

These principles help teach and remind kids to master what they can control, regardless of their circumstance.

In this book, we will follow the journey of Justin, a big fan of Stephen Curry, as he pursues greatness following his basketball dreams.

Justin faces many challenges along the way but uses WABA principles as a guide to success.

INTRODUCTION
STEPHEN CURRY

LATE AT NIGHT IN HIS BED, JUSTIN WOULD DREAM OF STEPHEN CURRY AND THE GOLDEN STATE WARRIORS. DREAMING OF THE WARRIORS WAS HIS FAVORITE WAY OF FALLING ASLEEP.

AFTER EATING HIS DINNER, HE WOULD BRUSH HIS TEETH, TAKE A BATH, AND RECALL ONE OF STEPHEN CURRY'S GREATEST GAMES.

TONIGHT, WOULD HE DREAM ABOUT GAME 5 OF THE 2015 NBA FINALS, WHERE HE SCORED 37 POINTS, ON THE WAY TO HIS FIRST NBA TITLE?

OR WOULD HE RECALL THE MAGICAL
MOMENTS OF THE 2022 NBA FINALS WHERE THE
WARRIORS WOULD WIN, AND CURRY WOULD BE NAMED
THE NBA FINALS MVP ?

THERE WERE MANY MAGICAL MOMENTS TO CHOOSE FROM.

WHILE JUSTIN'S DAD IS TOTALLY
SUPPORTIVE OF HIS SON'S LOVE FOR
BASKETBALL, HIS NUMBER ONE PRIORITY IS TO HELP HIS
SON DEVELOP A HEALTHY MINDSET FOR LIFE.

BE MINDFUL WITH YOUR WORDS

12

SUCCESS

EACH DAY AND NIGHT,
JUSTIN WOULD PRACTICE.

OFTEN TIMES HE WOULD TRY TO EMULATE STEPHEN
CURRY, BUT HE DID NOT HAVE THE SAME RESULTS.

HIS DAD WOULD OFTEN REMIND HIM,
"LEARNING THE FUNDAMENTALS IS
THE KEY TO SUCCESS."

"BUT THAT'S SO BORING!"
JUSTIN SAID.

15

JUSTIN SAID,
"WATCH THIS DAD!"
AS HE SHOT THE BALL FROM 40 FEET AWAY.

THE BALL CLANKED OFF THE BACKBOARD,
AND ROLLED DOWN THE STREET.

JUSTIN PUT HIS HEAD DOWN, SULKING, AND SAID TO
HIMSELF, "I'M NOT GOOD ENOUGH."

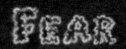

FEAR

The surrounding words: FAILURE, SADNESS, ANGER, EMPTINESS, DEPRESSION, INADEQUACY, LONELINESS, FRUSTRATION, INSECURITY, JEALOUSY, HELPLESSNESS, RESENTMENT, I CAN'T TRANSMUTE, OVERWHELM, GUILT

DAD WOULD QUICKLY JUMP IN AND REMIND JUSTIN,
"BE MINDFUL WITH YOUR WORDS."

"YOUR WORDS BECOME BELIEFS.
NEGATIVE BELIEFS TURN INTO NEGATIVE ACTIONS."

"YOU HAVE TO GUARD YOUR THOUGHTS, AND ONLY
ALLOW POSITIVE WORDS."

JUST LIKE HOW DRAYMOND GREEN
PLAYS ALL STAR DEFENSE FOR THE WARRIORS,
YOU HAVE TO DEFEND YOUR MIND."

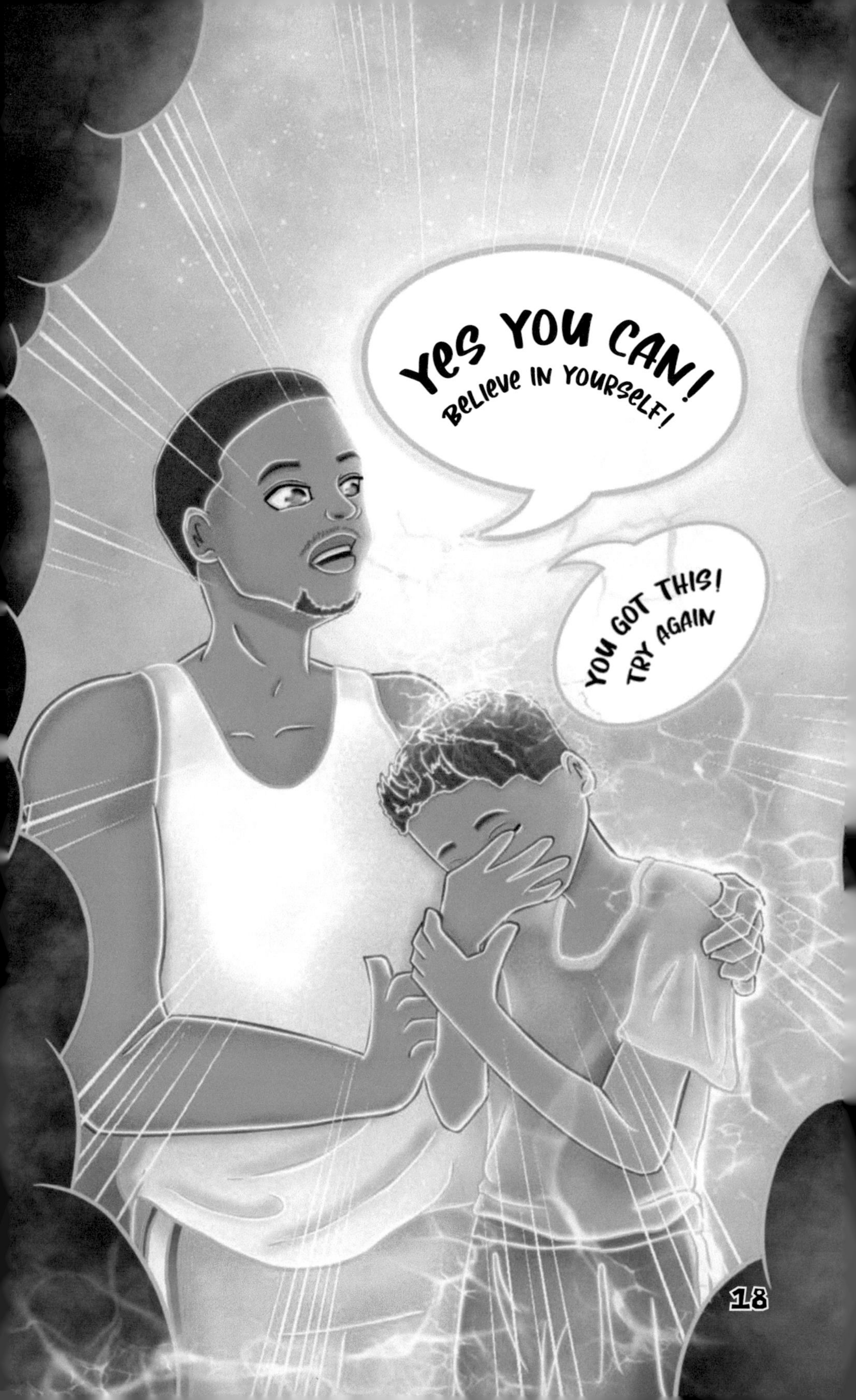
YES YOU CAN!
BELIEVE IN YOURSELF!
YOU GOT THIS!
TRY AGAIN

PLAY DEFENSE!

AFFIRMATIONS USE WORDS TO BUILD A STRONG MIND.

WHEN YOU SAY, "I AM,"

YOUR MIND IS CREATING THOUGHTS, ACTIONS,

AND SITUATIONS THAT REFLECT WHAT YOU SAY.

FEARLESS

SMART

SUPPORTED

DEDICATED

LEGENDARY

WRITE YOUR OWN AFFIRMATIONS, AND SAY THEM OUT LOUD EVERYDAY!

I AM _____

I AM _____

I AM _____

I AM _____

I AM _____

I AM _____

TAKE

ACTION

23

After teaching Justin the power of his words,
dad says,
"it's time to take action!"

"now that you have won the game
between your ears, lets do everything we can to
turn those beliefs into action!"

dad went on to explain,
"son, our minds have magical ways of turning our
dreams into reality through the power of our
belief in ourselves and others.
now lets get to work!"

I KNOW I CAN .

WITH A POSITIVE BELIEF IN HIMSELF,
JUSTIN BEGAN TO PRACTICE.

THIS TIME, HE USED THE POWER OF HIS
BELIEFS TO GUIDE HIM IN A MORE POSITIVE DIRECTION.

HE NO LONGER THOUGHT OF FUNDAMENTALS AS
"BORING".

HE ACCEPTED HIS DADS ADVICE WITH
A SMILE AND POSITIVITY.

PLAY OFFENSE!

HOW CAN YOU TURN YOUR POSITIVE THOUGHTS INTO ACTION?

_____

_____

_____

_____

_____

_____

DRAW YOURSELF TAKING ACTION

BE MINDFUL OF YOUR BEHAVIOR

SOON AFTER TAKING POSITIVE ACTIONS,
JUSTIN NOTICED THAT HIS GAME STARTED TO IMPROVE.

FOCUSING ON FUNDAMENTALS
NOT ONLY IMPROVED HIS GAME,
BUT MADE BASKETBALL EASIER AND MORE FUN.

JUSTIN'S DAD SOON NOTICED THAT
HIS BEHAVIOR STARTED TO CHANGE TOO,
BUT NOT ALWAYS IN A GOOD WAY...

AS JUSTIN BECAME BETTER AND BETTER AT BASKETBALL, HE WOULD OFTEN INTIMIDATE AND SAY NEGATIVE THINGS ABOUT HIS TEAMMATES.

SOMETIMES HE WOULD EVEN USE HIS SKILL ON THE BASKETBALL COURT TO BULLY OTHER KIDS.

JUSTIN'S DAD REMINDED JUSTIN THAT OUR BEHAVIOR MATTERS TOO.

Those who are blessed with great talent are also often given higher expectations as well.

Justin's dad explained,
"Playing basketball the right way is just as important as winning."

Being kind to his teammates and encouraging them was a fundamental skill in life --not just basketball.

LET'S PRACTICE!

Give some examples of positive behavior.

_____

_____

_____

_____

_____

_____

DRAW YOURSELF BEING KIND TO YOUR TEAMMATES.

A POSITIVE ATTITUDE ALWAYS WINS

40

As Justin grew older, he noticed that the competition got tougher, and he was no longer the best player on his team.

He was not the fastest, the best shooter, or the highest jumper, so at times this was discouraging.

Justin's dad offered his wisdom,
"On every team, there will be starters, reserves and coaches; but one thing that brings them all together is a positive attitude."

"Be positive no matter the position you play, and you will always win."

GREAT EFFORT JUSTIN!

JUSTIN HEEDED HIS DAD'S WORDS OF WISDOM
BY WORKING HARD AND DOING HIS BEST EVERYDAY.

THERE WERE GAMES WHEN HE PLAYED 30 MINUTES,
FOLLOWED BY GAMES WHERE HE SAT ON THE BENCH.

REGARDLESS OF THE SITUATION,
HE ALWAYS STAYED IN SHAPE, READY,
AND MOTIVATED WITH HIS NEW ROUTINE
AND HEALTHY POSITIVE OUTLOOK.

That year, Justin's team won the local little league basketball championship.

It was at this moment, that Justin discovered that the true joy in sports is being a part of a team.

46

PLAY OFFENSE!

LIST SOME EXAMPLES OF A WINNING ATTITUDE.

_____

_____

_____

_____

_____

_____

DRAW YOURSELF WINNING!

CONTROL YOUR WABA

JUSTIN LEARNED THAT WABA PRINCIPLES WERE NOT JUST FOR BASKETBALL. THEY COULD BE USED IN EVERY ASPECT OF HIS LIFE, INCLUDING SCHOOL!

BY FOLLOWING WABA PRINCIPLES, JUSTIN'S ACADEMIC PERFORMANCE GREATLY IMPROVED. UPON GRADUATING FROM HIGH SCHOOL, HE RECEIVED A FULL SCHOLARSHIP INTO A TOP UNIVERSITY IN THE COUNTRY.

HE CONTINUED TO PURSUE HIS DREAM OF MAKING IT INTO THE NBA UNTIL HIS DREAM FINALLY CAME TRUE!

YOUR DREAMS CAN COME TRUE TOO!
TRY WABA PRINCIPLES FOR YOURSELF! THEY WORKED FOR STEPHEN CURRY, JUSTIN, AND THEY WILL WORK FOR YOU TOO! FROM ONE LEGEND TO ANOTHER, WE BELIEVE IN YOU!

CONGRATULATIONS ON LEARNING HOW TO CONTROL YOUR
WABA! WELCOME TO THE HALL OF FAME!
DESIGN YOUR LEGENDARY JERSEY!

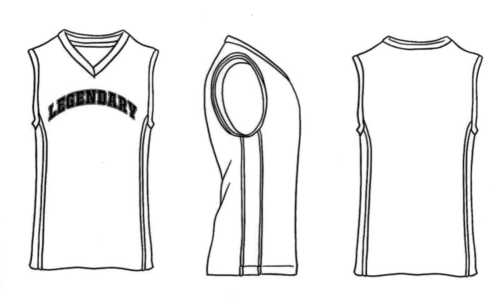

NOW THAT YOU HAVE MASTERED YOUR WABA, HOW WILL
YOU USE IT TO REACH YOUR DREAMS?

ABOUT THE AUTHOR

JEFFREY DEVINE

Jeffrey Devine, was born in Inglewood, California and raised in Long Beach.

He attended the University of California at Davis, where he received his degree in Computer Science.

After graduating, he went to work for Hewlett-Packard, where he worked for several years as a systems administrator and software developer.

Eventually, he went on to start his own business, Devine Consulting, Inc. which provides research, software development, and information technology support services.

Jeffrey is a huge fan of the Golden State Warriors. But the true love of his life is his family, including his wife Nurzedmaa, and kids Justin, Jackson, and Joy.

ABOUT THE ILLUSTRATOR

TIYE SAMONE

Tiye' Samone is a visionary and legendary advocate for positive representation, empowerment, education, and exponential lifestyle improvements within the Black community.

Tiye' has the Midas touch, and has flourished in every arena she has challenged herself to enter. She is a self-taught artist and illustrator with a burning passion to continue to exponentially grow in her skills and talents everyday.

In 2020, Tiye' founded Phase Creative Studios LLC to create opportunities for the Black community to mastermind creatively together.

She loves bringing joy, laughter, and fun to the creative process with a smile and sense of humor that is sure to put a smile on your face! Tiye' is creative, honest, and kind; and never hesitates to take initiative to speak life into herself, her projects, and even you!

DREAMS
DO
COME
TRUE

THANK
YOU!

WITH GRATITUDE FROM
FELLOW LEGENDS

55

Made in United States
Troutdale, OR
03/25/2024